ANGELS

for oliur
with all
my love

Marhn
X P   2006

ANGELS

Angels by Cecil Collins
First published in 2004 by Fools' Press
PO Box 43529, London SW15 6BW

A catalogue record of this publication
is available
from the British Library.

ISBN 0954440900

Printed by BAS Printers Ltd, Wiltshire

ANGELS
Cecil Collins

Compiled and edited
by Stella Astor

Fools' Press

LONDON

Contents

Illustrations

Foreword

Some years ago, I was responsible for a BBC documentary about Cecil Collins, which we called 'Fools and Angels'. For Cecil, the image of the fool, which he often painted, represents that in us which is open and childlike, that which is trusting and innocent and therefore vulnerable. It's the fool in us, he believed, which enables us to connect with the angelic world and with a reality that is invisible but nonetheless substantial. For this reason, angels are less easy to write about than fools, let alone to paint. One definition of an icon, which I have always liked, describes it as a window into heaven. Cecil's paintings of angels are for many people just that, a bridge into another reality.

There is of course a great danger in trying to pin down in words mysteries that can be communicated only in what Cecil calls 'the language of the inner life'. To learn this language demands effort, above all effort on oneself. One essential ingredient in our emerging humanity is, I believe, a sense of humour. Along with humility, it is what keeps things in proportion. Cecil loved a good joke and above all he could laugh at himself. His very appearance was an obvious target, with his rather shabby and ill-fitting overcoat, his ancient and battered trilby and his patched shirts. I think it's important for those who didn't know him to be aware of this aspect of his personality as they read the address which he gave in 1985 on the occasion of the unveiling of the windows he had designed. Cecil Collins was a deeply serious man, a dedicated artist and searcher for truth, but he could never be described as a fanatic.

In this address on angels, he was also at pains to point out how one-sided our modern culture and civilisation has become. In Cecil's view, the dominance of the masculine principle has been a major part of the problem, a dominance that has increasingly upset the subtle and delicate balance between the masculine and feminine principles within each of us. Here he was enormously helped by the companionship of his wife Elisabeth. She was not only on frequent occasions his model but was consistently his inspiration and an artist of merit in her own right.

For Elisabeth, her angel was extraordinarily real. Sometimes, when she was down in the dumps, she would say that her angel had probably gone on holiday. In reality, both she and Cecil knew very well that it is not the angels who leave us but we who move away from them. They are always there, ready to comfort and inspire, but we must be sufficiently open and sensitive to their presence for a communion to take place: cynics might say sufficiently foolish.

Jonathan Stedall
September 2002

Reflections

There is an experience which is common to everybody, although most people seem not to bother, an experience that the world is in some way permanent, eternal, of incredible purity . . .

I used to lie in bed in my bedroom as a child and look out of the window, there were these big white clouds . . . especially in April, and something about white clouds in this state of consciousness were doorways, gateways . . . something to do with the whiteness in the centre of these clouds which was reflected in the white counterpane on my bed . . .

I remember seeing this world in leaves growing off the side of walls as a child and in specks of dust lying on the ground in the backyard of my father's and mother's house, which seemed to show me that everything is permeated by this state of consciousness.

Cecil Collins: interview with Peter Fuller 1987

I began to see, early in my life, that the most important thing in life was that life was about consciousness, and I began to be aware that there was in us a potential of transformation of consciousness, that we were lazy and just let this thing lie, but we all of us have in us this potential to actually transform consciousness, and I became conscious in myself that this fact was the purpose of life, the real purpose of life . . . this was the object throughout all the great civilisations. It was the collective object behind all of them.

Cecil Collins: interview with Peter Fuller 1987

I began to see that our civilisation is really a tradesman's civilisation, with a tradesman's education and a tradesman's view of life and it is therefore a totally abnormal civilisation . . . our civilisation is the only known one in history not to be based on a metaphysical basis. We had great trade going on in the past but it was not the central theme. You can test a civilisation by what the big buildings are dedicated to . . . remember that great buildings of great civilisations were all focused on a metaphysical reality . . . I began to feel later on as an artist that, in some way, this is central to creativity.

Cecil Collins: interview with Peter Fuller 1987

My own art is concerned to give man peace and joy and harmony and to orientate his consciousness that he may have some experience of that great happiness which is forever, through the transmission of the mystery of love, through the mystery of beauty.

Cecil Collins: Hymn to Light
Ch4: Art, Faith & Vision 1989

What I believe in is what the ancients called giving man heart's ease, I believe that art should give man peace.

Cecil Collins: Hymn to Light
Ch4: Art, Faith & Vision 1989

When I got into the country, what helped me was this extraordinary silence and out of this silence came these pictures and I discovered knowledge takes the form of atmosphere, atmosphere as knowledge, a great discovery I think.

Cecil Collins: Hymn to Light
Ch4: Art, Faith & Vision 1989

Innocence for me is a very profound quality. Demonology is so popular and boring because it's so obvious but innocence is very profound.

Cecil Collins: Hymn to Light
Ch4: Art, Faith & Vision 1989

I'm not concerned with self-expression, I'm concerned with what I would call concentric imagination, that is imagination shared with the whole of mankind.

Cecil Collins: Hymn to Light
Ch4: Art, Faith & Vision 1989

I invented nothing really, the word original after all doesn't mean what it does to modern life . . . it means returning to the origins of images and the whole of my art is a return to the original world of creativity as manifest in universal images.

Cecil Collins: Hymn to Light
Ch4: Art, Faith & Vision 1989

An artist must give to the world what he can or what he must and some artists, who give the world torment, conflict, violence, are actually promoting this condition in the world and extending it. And that's a kind of betrayal.

Cecil Collins: Hymn to Light
Ch4: Art, Faith & Vision 1989

I believe that we live in a completely universal age now. We've got to grow up and accept universality. Universality is maturity and the Holy Spirit is one of the great images of universality.

Cecil Collins: Hymn to Light
Ch4: Art, Faith & Vision 1989

Brief Biography

Cecil Collins worked and taught in relative obscurity. Born in Plymouth in 1908, he won a scholarship to the Royal College of Art in 1927; there, he met the woman he was to marry, and with whom he shared the next sixty-two years of his life. In June 1936, he took part in the Surrealist Exhibition in London, but this was a movement to which he did not really belong. The show caused a stir and, in his own words, he was 'set up to become a whizz kid' yet he chose to put a lid on this success by turning away from the public eye to follow the path of his then unfashionable vision, that of a world infused with the numinous. He moved out of London and continued to paint, exhibit and sell his work while keeping in touch with other artists of similar inclination. It was through one such friendship that he moved to Devon, and became involved in the Art Studio which had been set up by Leonard and Dorothy Elmhirst, on their estate at Dartington.

Plagued by poor health he was unable to

join the war effort. Instead, as a form of service, he developed a method of teaching, that eventually evolved into something applicable to the essence of creativity in whatever form it takes. At the same time he began writing an essay, Vision of the Fool, published just after the war in 1947, a long and eloquent narrative about the state of awareness in each one of us that converses with the essence of life. Cecil Collins uses the Fool as a symbol for this.

The Fool, Collins tells us, is the element in everyone that restores and heals with fun; it is the magic that reawakens a sense of the wonder of life. The Fool is free from vested interest, untouched by the pride of cleverness and devoted to the sacredness of existence so he always experiences life as if for the first time. Bearing the creative gifts that can reshape and heal the degradation of a sterile society, conveying the regenerative quality that shares in life's joy and sorrow with compassion and simplicity, the Fool is as intangible as life itself. Society, blighted by a dislike for what it cannot capitalise or rationalise, disregards and exiles the Fool.

Collins, however, sees the real trouble in

society's absence of conscience. Conscience, he says, is the yardstick of a civilised society and, when it no long exists, ignorance rules and brutality pronounces the victories of the day. We live in an age that venerates the stewardship of a scientific technology, of efficiency and utility, over and above quality of life. Thereby, it effectively spoils poetic representations of life and a communion with the symbolic world. It depletes what Collins calls, 'the leisure of the soul'. He explains the hollowness that follows such deprivation. Society is obsessed by an unfulfilled bid to abate its enormous hunger. It is in the vortex of spiritual famine. And with little self-awareness, it wrongly believes it has found the horn of plenty when, in fact, it is merely the survivor of so-called progress. Moreover it will continue to squander its chances to engage with the regenerative secrets of life until its distintegration is complete. Then, and only then, will society crave resuscitation unless, by a miracle of creative effort, it can bring about a universal orientation towards an awakened conscience – this depends on the individual. He suggests that society could deepen its perception by slowing its pace and by entertaining and celebrating the Fool, for it is the Fool in one that touches the Fool in another.

Collins concludes this passionate essay by stating that the heart will be forever restless until it feeds from the lasting essence that is the very substance of each person, the essence that lies at the core of each person and the very fabric of life. For it is the expression of this part, whether useful or useless, which is the fact and the mystery of existence; and it is this part that will exist beyond all ideas, regardless of the most predominant trend in today's world, the depersonalisation of life.

In so saying, he was ahead of his time, and his words went largely unnoticed. Apart from this essay, little was generally known of Cecil Collins's ideas until after his death.

By contrast, his paintings and prints attracted a significant audience. The images in them emerge from the archetypal and symbolic world and reflect the inner life. The style is deliberately unrealistic in order to initiate a flow between the imagination and the subject matter. For some, his work evokes a recollection, the unceasing response to a timeless existence deep within each one of us, recognisable yet intangible. He viewed his pictures as stations of transmission; which he felt belonged to a new dawn, he knew he was living amidst cultural decay at the end of an era.

In 1970, Collins moved to London where he taught at the City Literary Institute and at the Central School of Art. He continued to teach until shortly before his death in 1989; and always stressed his paintings and his teaching were closely linked, each nurturing the other.

His teaching was innovative for its time, and its magic prompted great loyalty. In his life-drawing classes, he encouraged the study of technique in empathy with the model. At the same time, he aroused an awareness of a 'third power', *you have this* the invisible ingredient that gives vitality to creative work. His students used a wide range of traditional instruments; Chinese brushes and ink in various tones, quills, reed pens, chalk, charcoal and pencil, as well as fists and fingers. Sometimes they drew with both hands at once, either quickly or slowly: standing, sitting or kneeling, while holding the instruments in unusual positions. He taught them to develop and synchronise relationships between –

the instruments; the marks on the paper; and the atmosphere of the pose, together with 'poised attention' – and to respect and value the experience. It was not relaying the topography of the human form through measurement and analytic scrutiny, it was learning to converse from the heart, and to make this inner connection by first emptying oneself. He asked his students to look 'as if for the first time' without prejudice or manipulation, and to respond rather than react to what they saw.

Cecil Collins had a very clear understanding of the potency of the imagination and the role it plays in creativity. He understood it to be a tool for the transformation of human consciousness from the world of ignorance and darkness to the world of wisdom and light. He stressed that we should train and use the imagination, and not leave it to be ignored and abused. 'You become what you contemplate' he often remarked. He pointed out that in Greek tragedy murder and fornication always took place offstage, to watch it would 'offend the Gods'. He would incorporate sound and movement in his class;

he played music; sometimes he used recordings of the sea, the song of a lark or a passage from Plato. Full of surprises, he kept students on their toes, and kept reminding them that true creativity is about the transformation of consciousness.

The models were an integral part of these lessons. Starting off as eavesdroppers, they soon became witnesses of, and participants with, the teaching. They played a vital role, working hard to give short poses and movement imbued with a real sense of presence.

The drawings took off and bloomed along with the growing sensibility of the students. At once serious and enormous fun, Cecil's instruction was clear, yet demanded concentration. The students took what they were ready to receive and for most of them the class was a lasting inspiration and influence, with Cecil alerting them to the numinous qualities in art and in life. He also taught colour, correlating it with music, linking the students' approach to colour, and their response to harmony. He nurtured this response through the discipline and practise of mixing colour, and by encouraging paintings from the imagination

Amongst many exhibitions of his work, Cecil had retrospectives in London at the Whitechapel Gallery in 1959 (227 works), the Hamet Gallery in 1972 (62 works), the Tate Gallery in 1981 (42 prints), and at the Plymouth Art Centre in 1983 (40 works). He had a major retrospective at the Tate Gallery in 1989 (147 works), which continued for a short time after his death. During his life, collectors of his work included Kenneth Clark, Stephen Spender, John Trevelyan, Peter Pears and Benjamin Britten.

While the Tate Gallery houses a large, permanent collection of his work, he is widely represented in many smaller museums and galleries throughout Britain.

In the 1980s, I was lucky enough to become one of his many students. Eager to find out more, I set off, with a small cassette recorder, to the unveiling of the side windows at All Saints' Church in Basingstoke. These had been commissioned by Canon Keith Walker and executed in stained glass by Patrick Reyntiens from a design featuring angels by Collins, who had also been invited to speak on the subject.

Cecil spoke off the cuff in a deep, resonant voice. At one moment, just after he had referred to children, a baby gurgled. When he finished speaking, the choir gently broke into song. All this the little machine captured clearly. Cecil asked for the tape, and later lost it; luckily I had scribbled down its contents before handing it over.

Some twenty years later, rereading it inspired me to make his words available to a wider audience. I have edited them a little, without omitting or radically changing any of Cecil's sentences.

Stella Astor

Angels

I have been very kindly invited to say something about angels this morning, on the occasion of the unveiling of the windows. And I must say, it is with some trepidation that I take on this address because angels are a very difficult subject. Also I am well aware of the fact that there must be, in the church, many men of very high rank, theologians, who know far more about angels than I do. Fortunately, there are many ways to the spiritual life; the official way is not the only way. Christ himself has said, "... except that ye be as little children, you shall not enter the kingdom of heaven". This, I believe, is the vital statement about the perception of the spiritual world, the world of angels. I shall try and concentrate this address on that state of consciousness, that quality of consciousness, which perceives the angels. Again, I am not a theologian. I shall try and speak to you this morning as an artist, with all the defects of that point of view.

We live in a society where the angels and the divine world are not a normal part or a normal presence in our environment. Our environment is empty of them. It is empty of them for a very important reason, which is that our civilisation is the only one in the whole of the history of mankind, some 20,000 years, not to be based upon a metaphysical reality; that is, a reality which transcends biological man and that of the vested interests of the ego; a metaphysical reality which is unknowable, absolute, and yet a reality which can have a relationship with us, and we with it. Our civilisation therefore can be considered abnormal.

The scriptures say the spirit quickens and gives life, and the letter kills. The history of religious experience shows us religions are born of a vision and end as a formula, a crystallisation, a rationalisation.

This need to find security in rationalisation, in concept, and to justify by measurement and theology, appears to be a peculiarly masculine activity and as the masculine psychology has dominated and is dominating western civilisation, this contracted reductionism dictates all forms of education and is the main cause of the split in European man's nature: the split between the soul, the intellect, the heart and the body. This is the schizophrenic condition of modern man: a divided nature cannot see reality. What is more, our environment is empty of the spiritual world and this emptiness is characteristic of modern life.

Take away the warmth of human experience from the new scientific universe, and you have emptiness and meaninglessness; and this question of emptiness is very, very important; it makes us feel very alone. Our environment does not gather around us the family of the spiritual world of which the angels are part.

One of the main crises in our civilisation or rather one of the main causes of crisis, is the lack of feminine principle from our education, the feminine psychology: the loving, caring, affectionate and nourishing; the feminine genius for relationship, which is deep in the psychology of the feminine: the simultaneous, multi-dimensional nature of the feminine consciousness.

Relationship is the key because all creativity is concerned with relationship: the relationship of the stars to the sun, the sea with the shore. In our education we need now to re-discover our relationship and our friendship with nature, with organic life, our friendship with all created things. We need to rediscover our friendship with the divine world.

The angels are images of our relationship between that world and us. Biochemical man cannot see the divine world neither can psychological man see the divine world. It is what I might call the third man or the third woman in us, the third power in us, that woman and that man, who sees the divine world.

There is one period in all our lives when the third power is active in us and that is in our childhood when we experience virginity of consciousness, direct perception, seeing directly with the wholeness of consciousness before it is obscured by the conditioned mind. It is the conditioned mind that prejudges experience, so we never really experience anything, and this is a kind of prison, active in all fields of mental activity. This is the act of possessing and manipulating experience from the point of view of certain conditions and it withers the virginity of consciousness and experience becomes a mirage. Hence, Christ's statement, "accept that ye be as little children, to enter the kingdom of heaven". It was the great Indian saint Ramakrishna who said, speaking of those dark periods that you find in civilisations of the world, which the Hindus call Kaliyuga, I quote, he said "in those periods one does not hear the voice of God except in the mouth of a child, a madman, a fool or some such person".

In the great spiritual tradition of the Sufis there is a very ancient idea that in all our hearts there is an eye. And when this eye is shut we are asleep, we are sleepwalkers walking in the nightmare of the world.

All true culture and art, all good education and all good civilisations are really an education of the knowledge of the opening of the eye of the heart. This is the one great source of energy for education and for civilisation, and this brings us right to the centre of the problem, which is the return of the feminine psychology to education and religion and the rediscovery of the spiritual knowledge of the opening of the eye of the heart: the spiritual education of the heart. It is this eye that sees the world of the angels, for like sees like, like attracts like.

The language of the inner life can be translated into any other language, though certainly not into the surface relation of logic and reductionism, or the specialised knowledge of science. The language of the inner life is poetry, symbol image, dance, music and silence. It uses the musical language of analogy. It is the language of evocation. It is the knowledge and host of atmosphere, of climate as nuance. It is the language of the response to the wonder, the miracle and the mystery of life. It is in this language that the angels reveal themselves so that they become part of our environment.

Angels appear in most cultures of the world. To use an analogy of the fact that things work at different speeds, it is possible, I think, that angels live at a very high speed, higher than us, and that is why we call them invisible.

The angels are a wind; they are winged because they belong to the open skies of the spirit. They live in the oxygen of God. The angels are a wind force of divine mind. They are the spiritual intelligence that connects all worlds; they unify and they help transform our consciousness and our awareness. They are infused with the beauty of the divine world from which they come. Angels are essentially a being of the universality of the spiritual life; they redeem us from our selfish provincialism, our narrow tribal view of life.

The new discoveries in science show us that the world, the universe, is not just material as supposed by the nineteenth-century scientist. It is not in a way material at all. It appears to be made up of vibrations and atoms and the flow of vibrations. The crisis in modern science, it seems to me, is centred around the question, "What is the relationship of the human mind with these vibrations?" One of the most important indications that seems to arise from this crisis is the realisation that perhaps there are not two things, spirit and matter which are divided and in conflict, but different degrees of one reality: different degrees of vibrations on a scale from the lower end of vibrations we call matter to the higher, the vibration and radiance of the world of light which is the world of angels. We see according to our place on the scale of vibrations. This seems to me to throw a lot of light on the whole question of the experience of the spiritual world.

According to traditional knowledge, man is placed in a critical position on the continuum of existence. Critical because he is placed between the demonic world and the angelic world and both these worlds are reflected in him. Civilisations are subject to psychic rhythm and seasons. At the end of a cycle of civilisation, man forgets the true meaning and significance of his life and becomes no longer spiritually educated; his inner defences are weakened; the forces of the demonic world are able to penetrate him; and take over his life by hypnotising him, confining him to the prison of biological existence, influencing and forming his education, his culture. All this is clearly shown in much modern art in which the demonic plays a very large part.

I quote from traditional knowledge, "man is a very important cosmic instrument and he has a very important task. Man's real purpose is being an instrument of transformation: for transforming the raw, dark energy of the demonic world to the radiant light of the angelic world, the transformation from the world of darkness into the world of light." That is the real purpose of man's existence, both individually and collectively. This transformation should manifest in education, art, culture and civilisation. Transformation therefore is the key to the mystery of human consciousness.

Traditional knowledge shows that the first step towards this transformation is for man consciously to turn towards the world of light. This is called orientation and it is just here that the archetypal image of the angel comes into focus. The angel is a mediator between us and the world of light and in certain traditions the angel is called the companion of light.

The windows in a building are instruments of light. One can see the religions of the world are like different windows through which the divine light shines. They are all different colours but the divine light has no colour, its universality gives light to all colours. The divine light is not the colour of any particular religion, although all colours bear witness to, and manifest, that light. Hence, divine light is the realisation of this spiritual fact, and there is no room for quarrelling and dissension and for all those terrible crimes that have disfigured and mutilated man's religious history and destroyed man's consciousness of the divine: a history of cruelty that has caused the angels to weep, to weep and to weep, as they wept at the crucifixion of Christ.

Turning away from the dark narrow prison of collective religious egotism that is destruction of life, we look into the clear air of universality and we see that the angels are countless bodies of light in the odes of eternity. They are the signs and the witnesses of a secret relationship, a secret friendship between us and the divine world. They are an awareness of a new life, a new consciousness: the birth of love, the dawn of consciousness.

There is in each one of us, an unconscious angel of dawn, of first being, of life. In the Koran it says, "yes indeed we created man and we know what whispers in his soul".

Far beyond the world of answers and explanations, far beyond the world of reason and logic, far beyond all expediency and utility, who can fathom the depths and the mystery of the human heart, with its great longing? Who can fathom the mystery of the radiance of the Angels who are filled with the great happiness and the world of eternal light?

. . . there is undoubtedly a vision born in people, I'm sure of it, a new vision . . . like all new visions you cannot give people anything, you can only awaken what they already know.

Everything is already in us now.

Cecil Collins: Hymn to Light
Ch4: Art, Faith & Vision 1989

Acknowledgements

Thanks to the following people for their
help and contributions:
Raphael Block, Hugh Bredin, Lily Corbett,
Ginger Gilmour, Sylvie Leboulanger,
Harry Marshall, Muriel Maufroy, Jonathan Stedall,
Christopher Webster and Jo Winsloe.

A thank you also to Ruth Eisenhart,
Jeremy Gale and Maria Lancaster for their support
and encouragement.

Thanks to Cecil and Elizabeth Collins for their
warmth, humour
and guiding intelligence.

Bibliography

Anderson, William. *Cecil Collins The Quest for the Great Happiness.* London: Barry and Jenkins, 1988.

Collins, Cecil. *Cecil Collins The Vision of the Fool and other writings.* Ipswich: Golgonooza Press, 1994.

Collins, Cecil. *Cecil Collins Meditations, Poems, Pages from a Sketchbook.* Ipswich: Golgonooza Press, 1997.

Collins, Cecil. *The Vision of the Fool and other writings, enlarged edition.* Ipswich: Golgonooza Press, 2002.

Collins, Judith. *Cecil Collins A retrospective exhibition.* London: The Tate Gallery, 1989.

Fools' Press